I0758123

Untethered Love

A Chronicle of Grief and Medical Mystery

A true story

E.W. Borgoyne
ewborgoyne@hotmail.com

Copyright © 2021 E.W. Borgoyne
All rights reserved.
ISBN: 9798755617758

DEDICATION

To my soulmate Kathy

ACKNOWLEDGMENTS

I want to thank all of my friends and family for their unwavering support during one of the most challenging times in my life.

In particular, I want to thank my long-time friend Carol Gibbs for instilling in me the strength of serenity to accept things I cannot change. Carol sent me this book which has helped me in my grieving process. Many of the ideas in this book are integrated into my story.

I also want to thank my Sister-in-Law Sandi Banta for encouraging me to write this story.

FORWARD

What happened? How are you doing? These are the most common questions that my friends, family, and acquaintances have asked me over the past few months. But how do you answer them when you have the same questions? Searching for answers has been a recursive process for me. I walk through the timeline of events in my mind, and for each event, I ask why. After coming up with a plausible answer, I take what I've learned and repeat the entire process.

What happened to my wife Kathy remains a medical mystery. Yes, we know the cause of death and some of the contributing reasons. But we don't know the actual root cause—what ultimately triggered the chain of events leading to her death. The cochlear implant surgery six weeks earlier seemed to be the leading candidate. But correlation is not causation.

As to how I am doing, the answer is tightly bound to the first question. My mental state during the time Kathy was in intensive care is different than it is now, indeed. There were few answers during those critical few weeks. Although questions remain, I searched for answers, and telling the story has been healing for me.

'Grief must be externalized .. Telling the story helps to dissipate the pain." *On Grief and Grieving.*

PROLOGUE

The timeline in this story is based on text messages, photos, emails, phone call logs, and credit card records. I tell the story based on what was known at the time, including recollection of my thoughts and words and what I recall others have said to me.

I gave much thought to whether to share some of the unflattering pictures of Kathy. In the end, I felt it was essential to understand the ups and downs she was experiencing during her ordeal.

After receiving the medical records from Dignity Health, I added details that I did not know at the time.

These details are shown in boxed texts like this.

CHAPTER 1

Till death do us part

Friday, June 4th, 2021

I sat with Kathy most of the day. I gently held her hand, told her that I loved her and not to be afraid. She stared expressionlessly in whatever direction her head was pointing. I prayed that she could hear me. I prayed that she wasn't suffering.

She held her arms up as though she was hugging someone. Her fists were tightly clenched. At one point, she lifted one leg high above the bed as if she was exercising. The softness of her skin and plumpness of her body from constant IV treatment at the hospital was no longer present. She was starving and dehydrating to death before my eyes. It didn't seem right, but this is the path we both chose for ourselves. This is what we told our children and was clearly stated in the medical power of attorney.

I waited for a family friend to come by after work for a visit. Her presence was most comforting for me, and I'm sure for Kathy as well. Before leaving, she whispered in Kathy's ear, "It's ok to let go."

Her breathing was becoming more and more erratic, and the Hospice nurse positioned Kathy's head to a more comfortable position. I didn't want to leave her alone, but I was exhausted and hungry.

I got home, poured myself a glass of wine, took a few tokes of Kathy's medical weed, and started to rummage through the freezer. Just then, my cell phone rang, and 'Hospice' appeared on the screen. The night nurse said my wife had taken a turn for the worse; I knew her death was imminent. My only hope was there was still time to see her one last time.

Against my better judgment, I got back into my car and began to drive. "Hang on, baby. Don't leave me yet!" I cried out as I did my best not to get into an accident. Tears clouded my eyes and the effects of the wine and weed caused me to question the route back. For a moment, I wasn't sure what road I was supposed to turn on. "oh yeah, Dobson Road," I remembered.

Suddenly I felt a pulse of energy pass through me—I knew that Kathy's soul had left her body.

As I parked the car, I got another call from Hospice that confirmed what I already knew. I answered my phone and said I was in the parking lot and would be there in seconds. The nurse met me as I ran towards Kathy's room and held my arm. She told me to be careful not to move her. It's what the state medical board required pending an investigation.

I planted my face in the pillow on which she laid her head and sobbed. I don't remember the exact words the nurse was saying to me, but they had a calming effect. Suddenly I felt at peace. "I want to be alone with my wife for a while," I said to the nurse, and she left.

I sat in the chair next to Kathy on the other side of her bed and called each of my children and other family members to give them the news. I sat there for what seemed to be a very long time. I was numb and thought that I might be dreaming. I reached over to touch Kathy's face to feel the remaining warmth of her body before it drained out forever.

I thought about the events of the past three weeks. I was angry at the countless doctors that were involved in her case but couldn't save her. They couldn't even provide a root cause. Was it the cochlear implant, the COVID shot, or was it something else? I was angry at myself for not doing more sooner and for the selfish emotions I had felt. I thought about what the future would be for myself and my family. And I thought about my next steps.

Untethered Love

After a final kiss on her forehead, I left Kathy for the very last time and returned home to try to figure things out.

CHAPTER 2

Kathy's hearing began to degrade sometime around 2008. We had just moved from the flatlands of Phoenix to a mountainside home in the mile-high community of Pine, Arizona. The altitude affected her migraines, and we thought it might be affecting her hearing as well. She had trouble hearing certain voices and was experiencing Tinnitus—a stressful ringing in the ears.

Her mother had depended on hearing aids for several years, and Kathy worried it might be hereditary. An audiology exam showed her hearing loss in the lower frequencies, which helped explain why some voices in the lower range were hard for her to hear—especially men. She started using a hearing aid, and this improved her hearing for a while. Eventually, it grew worse, and she went to a hearing specialist, Dr. Mark Syms.

Kathy was diagnosed with otosclerosis, where abnormal bone growth occurs around the stapes bone (or stirrup). This caused the small bone to become frozen and unable to vibrate and send sounds to the inner ear—a conductive hearing loss. It was not only genetic but pregnancy was considered a risk factor and it predominantly affected white women. It was a perfect storm.

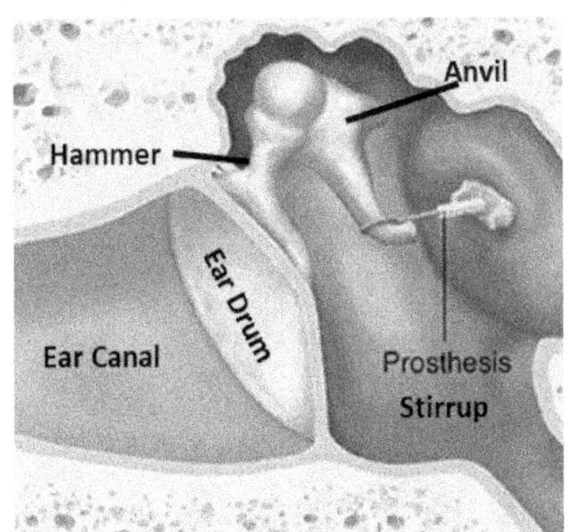

The solution was to implant a stapes prosthesis replacing all or part of the original stapes bone allowing the sounds to reach the cochlea. The outpatient procedure was performed on Kathy's left ear in December 2014 and produced immediate improvements. Then it was done in her right ear in May of 2015.

...

Eventually, her hearing began to degrade again. By this time, we had left our home in Pine and moved back to the Phoenix area. But her migraines continued to worsen, and she applied for a medical marijuana card.

Her degraded hearing and severe migraines caused her to avoid social settings. This led to depression.

CHAPTER 3

By April of 2019, Kathy had her hearing checked every couple of months, and it was getting worse. I would sit outside the soundproof booth and hear her responses, or lack thereof, to the words she was supposed to repeat. The graphs in the audiology report displayed visually what we already knew.

"Your right ear is 'profoundly' deaf to the human voice in the range of 100 and 300 Hz. Even with higher frequency sounds, your ear is considered 'severely' deaf," Dr. Syms explained. "Your left ear is not much better, rated 'moderate to severely deaf.'"

"So, the stapes operation won't work again?" Kathy asked

"No, the problem is in the inner ears itself—sensorineural hearing loss," he explained.

The cochlea wasn't doing its job even if the conductive process involving the stirrup bone was working. The tiny hairs inside the cochlea that respond to the auditory stimulus from the stirrup weren't working. It was a common age-related problem but accelerated if there was a genetic tendency. It was the gift from Kathy's mother that kept on giving.

"What are my options?" Kathy asked anxiously.

"A cochlear implant would be the next option," he said.

I knew a little about these devices after listening to Rush Limbaugh talk about his experiences. He was the most prominent person I knew who used them and wore one in both ears.

"We'll have to begin the approval process, which requires certain criteria to be met. But in the near term, you might consider a crossover device," Dr. Syms explained. "The hearing aid in your right ear serves no purpose since you are deaf in that ear."

E.W. Borgoyne

A crossover device looks like a regular hearing aid. But, instead of amplifying the sound in the ear, it relays the sounds to the other hearing aid using Bluetooth. This would allow her to hear sounds on the right side of her head in her left ear—the only auditory connection to the outside world, and *it* was in poor condition.

The crossover worked better than we expected. I thought Kathy would be confused by sounds she heard in her left ear coming from the right side, but she adapted well. However, tinnitus was becoming more and more severe, and it was interfering with her ability to distinguish from normal sounds. She would talk very loudly to get over the noise she was experiencing in her head.

I began to do more research on cochlear devices. It seemed to be the only long-term solution—the last chance for everyday life.

CHAPTER 4

I love you, Grandma

The cochlear implant system includes the external device and the implant. The external device is fundamentally different than a traditional hearing aid.

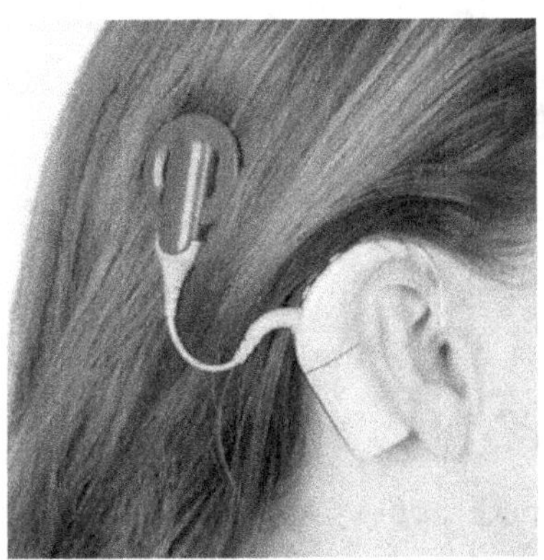

A sound processor is worn on the back of the ear. A small microphone loops over the front of the ear and picks up sounds that would typically enter the ear canal. The loop is secured to an ear hook that keeps the processor in place. The sound processor connects by wire to the headpiece that magnetically attaches to the implant. The digitized sound signals are transmitted to the implant device receiver under the skin. The ear canal is completely bypassed.

The implant requires an outpatient surgical procedure. The surgeon cuts into the skin behind the ear and then opens the mastoid bone—a pyramid-shaped bone just behind the ear. Navigating around the facial nerves, the surgeon creates an opening to access the cochlea. The electrode array is inserted and coiled into the cochlea. The surgeon then places the implant device receiver under the skin behind the ear, securing it to the skull.

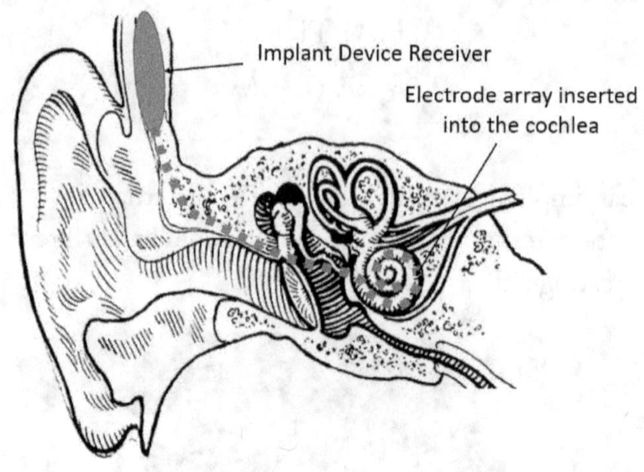

The electrode array stimulates the nerves directly without involving the cochlear hairs. Fundamentally, the human analog hearing system is converted to digital.

Like many medical devices, this does not have a sticker price. Estimates range from $30,000 to $50,000 depending on accessories. Medicare will only pay for one; the second one is on you if you want it.

Dr. Syms noted that the device manufacturers enjoy most of the profits, while the surgeons only get a small fraction. "Boo-hoo," I thought to myself.

...

"I love you, Grandma," said Eli. He waited patiently for a response. "Kathy!" I yelled out. "Eli is trying to tell you something!" She quickly snapped out of her silent world, turned toward him, and smiled. "I love you too, Eli!" she shouted to him. I could feel the frustration she was experiencing, and it made me sad.

In public, she depended on lip-reading to help fill the gaps in her hearing. But everyone was wearing masks because of the COVID pandemic and made this impossible. They created more problems since they sometimes unknowingly flicked the hearing aid from her ear.

Kathy recalled when her mother was alive would often smile and shake her head in agreement to whatever the other person was saying to her. This is where Kathy was as well. I knew it was so embarrassing, and I felt heartbroken.

With all the things going on in the world and her own life, she told me she was "tired of living." I wanted so badly to fix her problems and make the pandemic go away. I just wanted my wife to be happy again.

By the fall of 2020, Kathy was approved for the cochlear device. We made an appointment with Lindsay at Dr. Sym's office to learn more.

CHAPTER 5

November 2020

Lindsay showed us a couple of PowerPoint presentations explaining the surgical procedure, risks, outcomes, and rehabilitation. It was pretty technical information that I was familiar with from my research, and Kathy asked some excellent questions.

I asked about losing the device, especially with having to wear masks. Seems it would be more difficult with the wire and attachment. Lindsay laughed and told us a story where one of her patients lost the device when it suddenly attached itself to a metal doorway. Kathy and I looked at each other without expression.

Patient expectations were the most crucial factor, the presentation emphasized. 'You will have to learn how to use the implant. This will take time and effort.' It said. 'Cochlear implants are instruments. Getting one is like buying a violin. Just because you have a violin does not mean you know how to play one. Just because you get a cochlear implant does not mean you can hear with the cochlear implant.'

"What does that mean?" Kathy asked suspiciously.

"It means you are going to have to work hard over the next several months to learn and adjust," replied Lindsay, then pointing back to the presentation.

'Initially, what you hear will sound funny or weird. Some say that voices sound like Mickey Mouse, chipmunks, or robotic like R2D2,' the presentation read.

"You have to be committed and put in the effort," Lindsay said.

After living together for over forty-five years, I knew from the expression on Kathy's face what she must be thinking. "Am I willing to put that kind of effort into this? What choice do I have?" The decision was entirely Kathy's to make, not like a joint decision to get married, have children, buy a house or a new car. Of course, I would be there to help and support her.

This was not the time for final decisions, though. There was more work to be done.

"What about MRIs," I asked. "I heard that some cochlear devices are dangerous."

"All the brands are approved 'MRI Conditional,' meaning there are certain instructions that must be followed."

She gave us information on three vendor options: Advance Bionics, Cochlear, and Med-El. "Dr. Syms won't make a recommendation," she said. We thought it was strange.

"When I had my hip replacement surgery, the doctor didn't give me vendor options," I said, expecting some sort of response.

Lindsay told me to research all three manufacturers and make a decision. The material we were given was marketing brochures, highlighting their strong points and bashing the competitors. We were to review all documentation and return for device selection and additional counseling before surgery.

At home, Kathy and I looked at brochures and other information that was provided. It was confusing, and after a few weeks, she contacted Lindsay to ask her what the next step was. She told us to follow the checklist. There was no checklist in our packet.

December 2020

We returned to meet with Lindsay to ask more questions. I asked about one vendor who warned that the length of the electrode array was critical and could cause damage. "It doesn't matter at all," she said confidently. "Doesn't matter?" I thought. Why bother researching this with all the conflicting and insignificant information out there.

"So, what is the next step?" we asked. "Look at the checklist," she responded.

I showed her the folder we had, and there was no checklist. Without a word, she pulled a blank one from her file and began checking off the items we completed. Pointing to the unfinished actions, "Need to get a CT scan and have her primary doctor sign off on the surgery. Then make an appointment for a pre-op review."

I'm always amazed how some people, whose job is to help others navigate a process for the first time, act as if we should already know what they know.

January 2021

Thank goodness 2020 is behind us. With the vaccine now released, it seemed that there was hope, at last, to get this COVID thing behind us. Time to look forward with renewed hope.

The winter is the best time of the year in Phoenix, Arizona. It's the reward full-time residents receive for living through the hellish summer months. Kathy and I loved to sit outside on the front patio, share a bottle of wine, and talk about our plans.

"Promise me that this will be the last summer I have to spend in Arizona," Kathy said to me. The summer of 2020 was incredibly hellish, with an extended period of days over 115 degrees. Cacti were falling over, and palm trees were dying.

"I can't promise you that, but I'll try to come up with a plan," I said.

I knew she was disappointed that we had to let our house go up in Pine. She loved it up there and hoped we could buy a smaller place in the cool pines again someday.

We made plans to go to Florida with our grandsons this upcoming July. We stayed at a place in Sarasota called the Lime Tree Resort. We'd gone there many times with our children. This time we would spend some quality time with just the four of us.

We kept dragging our feet to avoid making a final decision. Yes, we; this wasn't a decision Kathy wanted to make alone. She depended on me to push her off the fence. I didn't blame her because I didn't envy her. It was a frightening prospect to know that you would permanently lose your hearing in one ear, even though you were almost there anyway.

We decided to go forward with the implant so Kathy would have time to recover for our Florida vacation.

CHAPTER 6

January 27th, 2021

We knew it was inevitable. "Sissy," our Jack Russel Terrier's health had been going downhill. We had to put our other two senior dogs down late last year. This was hard for Kathy, and she cried for days. I hoped this would be the last of her bad news for a while.

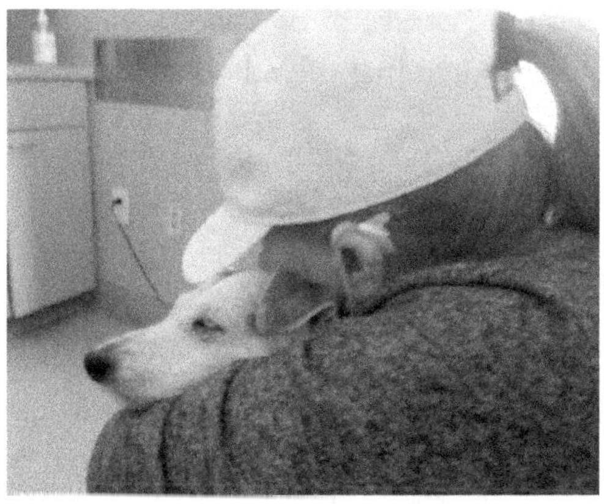

March 24th, 2021

We returned for counseling with Lindsay. Kathy said she was nervous about the surgery. "Will I be ok for the vacation in Florida in July?" She asked.

"You'll be fine," Lindsay said. "So, which vendor did you choose?"

"I don't remember which one," Kathy replied. "Whichever one I put in the checklist."

"You chose Advanced Bionics. So why did you choose them?"

The questions felt like an interrogation, but I could appreciate why she was doing that. It was to make sure we were confident we made the right choice. I began to think that we didn't investigate the options enough. But it was just a lot to digest.

"I guess it was the accessories they offered," Kathy said.

The list of options and accessories to choose from was overwhelming. There were different colors, power supplies, carrying cases, cables, the list went on. The options were included in the package, along with the choice of two accessories. Advanced Bionics offered what Kathy wanted that the others didn't.

The 'TV Connector' accessory streamed audio from the television or other media devices directly into the device. No more depending on subtitles that never seemed to be in sync with the dialog. The 'Partner Mic' accessory was a remote microphone allowing someone to talk without yelling. She would be able to hear grandchildren say, "I love you, grandma," and she would hear me when I said, "I need another cup of coffee, Baby." Hey, it was our deal—I made the coffee, and Kathy would fill the cups!

With the options and accessories decided, we reviewed the risks outlined in the consent form.

"This procedure may result in: bleeding; numbness or stiffness about the ear; taste disturbance; increased Tinnitus; neck pain; skin reactions; and leakage of inner ear fluid, which may result in meningitis. Spinal fluid drainage can result in meningitis. This is a remote possibility and would require further treatment in the hospital. Electrical stimulation (within the cochlea) may result in increased Tinnitus, facial nerve stimulation, dizziness, or pain, etc."

"Oh, great," Kathy sighed, looking at me. It seemed to me these were just specific warnings you might expect with any type of surgery. I shrugged my shoulders, then she signed the consent.

Untethered Love

A few days later, Kathy lost her crossover device, probably when she took her mask off. It didn't matter, really, since she would be having the cochlear device implanted in that side.

But with a flick of the mask, her hearing instantly degraded, and a thousand-dollar medical device was gone for good. Was this the way it was going to be?

CHAPTER 7

April 15th

The cochlear implant surgery was scheduled for 11 am at the St. Joseph's Hospital outpatient surgery facility. I dropped Kathy off and parked the car. I wasn't allowed in the facility due to COVID restrictions, so I went across the Street to the cafeteria, had some lunch, and waited for the call.

Around 2:30, I got the call that the operation was complete. I picked up the car and drove to the same place I dropped her off. They gave us a large backpack containing the external device and accessories. They told us to bring it to the follow-up appointment next week.

We couldn't get over the size of the backpack for such a small device.

The right side of Kathy's head was bandaged. "Take a picture of me," she said. "I want to send it to the kids."

Friday, April 23rd

Today Kathy's device was going to be enabled. We were optimistic and forgot what Lindsay told us that it would take time to learn how to listen. We brought the backpack with us that contained the external device and all the accessories.

There was a strict protocol at Dr. Syms's office requiring masks and plastic gloves. We had no choice but to bring our grandchildren with us. Eli had a nasty cough, which understandably got the attention of everyone there. We waited just outside the fitting area, so I couldn't hear what Lindsay was saying to Kathy.

They inspected the incision area and found no concerns. "Healing can take up to 6 months," Lindsay explained. She then set up the MAPs processor with Kathy's iPhone. MAPs are programs that help optimize the cochlear implant user's access to sound by adjusting the input to the electrodes on the array implanted into the cochlea.

"I wish my husband was here," Kathy laughed nervously.

Lindsay then explained the care and maintenance, how to put on the device, change batteries, change programs, and volume. Kathy was overwhelmed.

"You should wear the device during all waking hours, taking a one-hour break as needed for comfort," Lindsay explained. "Get familiar with all the parts of the speech processor. At the next appointment, we'll pair the accessories with the implant and explain their use."

Kathy came into the room where I was sitting with the grandkids. Dr. Syms had just scolded me for bringing them down and not to do it next time. I couldn't blame him for being upset. Eli was coughing and running around, but we had no choice.

"How did it go?" I asked Kathy. I knew from the look on her face that she was stressed out.

...

Untethered Love

She missed the follow-up exam the following Thursday, April 29th, because she got the day confused.

Monday, May 3rd

Kathy tried to follow the directions she was given, but it wasn't going very well. She wrote to Dr. Syms on the patient portal.

"I have had this device for less than two weeks. In that time, I've developed headaches while wearing my cochlear implant. These headaches turned into migraines which I have a history of. It's been 5 days since I have worn my implant because of the headache. The medication I've been taking has minimal effects. Any advice as to what I can do. I am not learning to use my cochlear implant if I am not wearing it. Thank you for your time."

He wrote back, *"You need your headaches managed. Please see neurology or primary care. The implant should not cause migraines."*

I could see how frustrated Kathy was. Her last hope for hearing was causing her grief and disappointment. I tried to imagine what that would be like. It must be a lonely feeling. I wanted to support her as much as I could.

Friday, May 7th

Her frustration continued. "Read this note I'm going to send to Dr. Syms," Kathy said to me. "Does it make sense to you?"

"Recently, I related having the cochlear implant causing headaches. I have gotten my headaches under control, but the headaches rebound as soon as I use my implant causing pain and vomiting. I think the distortion is so loud that it is an assault on my brain. By the afternoon, I have to remove it just to have a much-needed rest. My appointment isn't till May 18th. I am not sure how to proceed. Should I still wear it despite the overbearing loudness, or wear it sparingly. I've tried turning it down, but the voices are too low. I realized headaches are rare, but I seem to be the exception. Please advise. "

E.W. Borgoyne

"That's perfect," I said. "Send it."

Later that day, she got a response from Lindsay. *"Wear the implants as much as possible. I wish you could have made your last appointment to address some of these issues, but I do not have any openings until your next appointment. Please try to reduce the amount of background noise you are in and wear the device as much as possible."*

Dr. Syms added, *"Your description indicates your migraines are not under control. Wear the implant as much as you can tolerate. The less you wear it, the longer it will take to tolerate it."*

Kathy's frustration was through the roof, and I felt helpless.

CHAPTER 8

Saturday, May 8th

I made the appointment to get the vaccine weeks in advance. That's when there was a high demand. Kathy followed my lead on the decision to get the shot and wasn't too concerned. She always got a flu shot every year. We got the COVID vaccine at the Walgreen down the Street.

Sunday, May 9th

It was Mother's Day. Kathy wasn't feeling well, so we canceled our plans to go out for brunch. I got her a dozen roses like I usually do.

"My head is killing me," she said. "I need to go to Urgent Care." We thought it might have something to do with the COVID shot. We went to Urgent Care, and they gave her a cocktail of Benadryl and something else.

That seemed to help her for the rest of the day and into the following day, Monday.

Tuesday, May 11th

I had a 10 am doctor appointment, and before I left, Kathy said she needed to go to the emergency room. I suppose I was numb from hearing her complain so much about her headaches; I told her, "As soon as I get back, we'll go."

I got a text from Kathy at 10:40, "Hurry, I'm Dying."

When I got home, Kathy was complaining of severe migraines nausea, and she was vomiting. The pain had gotten much worse since Sunday—Mother's Day.

"You have to take me to the emergency," she said to me. "Why don't you want to take me?" she cried out after I asked her a few dumb questions.

The emergency department at Mercy Gilbert Medical Center was busy when we checked in the early afternoon. I called Eli's school and told them I wouldn't be able to pick him up at the regular 2 pm time, then I called Kaili's paternal grandmother and arranged to pick her up at school.

After being admitted, Kathy was assigned to a bed in a hallway since all the beds were assigned. I found it comforting that we are taking serious action on these headaches plaguing Kathy for several weeks. We chatted, and I read a book that I brought with me as we waited for answers.

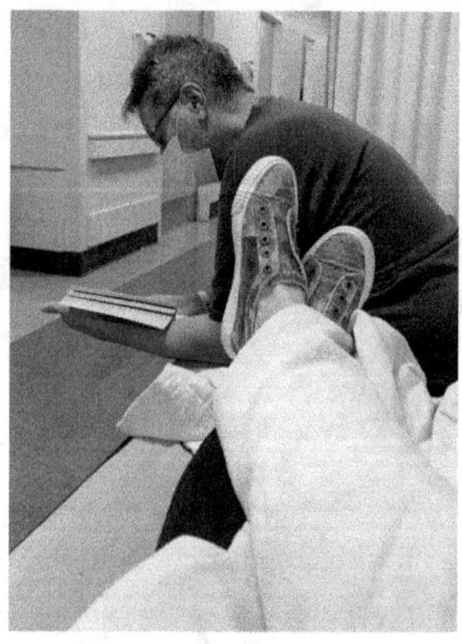

Her initial exam was benign, and the lab results were "unremarkable." They suspected either the COVID vaccine (25% of patients report headache post-vaccine) or the positioning of her implant. They ordered a CT scan to look at the implant area.

I felt Kathy was in good hands. She was given a cocktail of Compazine, Benadryl, and Decadron, which made her feel better. They considered discharging her to go home with outpatient neurology follow-up if the CT scan looked normal. But it was far from that.

The CT scan revealed "bilateral subacute subdural hematomas," and a tear around the implant site. "Did you recently bump your head?" The doctors asked Kathy. "No," she told them.

Her condition was considered "Guarded," They decided to transfer Kathy to St. Joseph's Hospital and Barrow Neurological center. They contacted Dr. Syms for him to follow up after she arrived there. They moved her to a gurney for transfer by ambulance.

Kathy was happy that she was getting the attention she believed she needed. My emotions were mixed. It was a good thing she was going to the top neurological hospital in Arizona. Still, at the same time, the situation was becoming more serious. I was angry at myself for delaying my decision to get Kathy into the emergency room.

I called my sons Ryan and Scot to let them know what was going on.

CHAPTER 9

I stopped by the house to pick up Kathy's tablet and other things before meeting her at the hospital. As I drove down to St. Joseph's, I began to digest what was going on.

The rear entrance to St. Joseph's on 3rd Avenue across from the parking garage was closed for construction. This was where I entered, just one month earlier, while waiting for Kathy's implant procedure. A medical van driver told me to go around the building to the front entrance. All I had to do was go to the second floor of the garage, where there was a visitor center, then cross the pedestrian bridge.

Instead, I walked around to the north side emergency entrance, where they told me to go around the south side then to the west side. While I was on my hike, Kathy called to tell me what floor she was on. I was sweating when I finally reached the main entrance.

She was smiling when I entered her room in the ICU. But the look on Kathy's face seemed to ask the question, "what kind of a mess have I gotten into this time?"

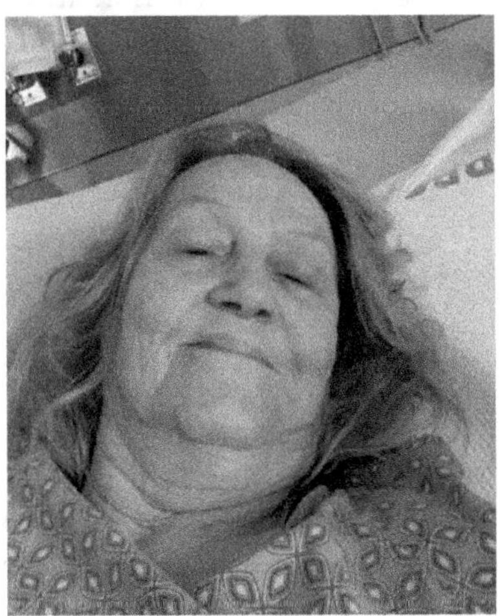

The doctors asked the same questions as they did at Gilbert. "Did you bang your head anytime recently?" Neither of us could remember that happening. Visiting hours were over at 8 pm, so I had to leave. I gave her the tablet and medication from home—which was a 'no-no.' Kathy and I kissed goodnight, and I told her I would be back tomorrow.

The hallways in St. Joseph's Hospital ran 45 degrees with the Neuroscience Tower where Kathy was located. It was disorienting, but I realized how close the parking garage was once I got my bearings and found my way. It would still take several days to navigate the hallways without getting lost. I called Ryan as I was driving out of the parking garage and gave him an update. Scot called and said he was coming down in the morning.

At home, I began to research Kathy's condition. A hematoma is a bruise deep under the skin and can occur anywhere in the body. The bruise is caused by some impact on the body, which causes blood vessels to break, allowing blood to pool. When the bruise is on the head, where the scalp is thin, the skull transfers the shock from an impact into the meninges, the brain's protective layer. Within the meninges is a space that contains Cerebro-Spinal Fluid (or CSF) that helps the cushioning effect. A subdural hematoma occurs when so-called bridging veins are ruptured in this space and pool into globs. It's essentially a brain hemorrhage.

Kathy's was bilateral, meaning one on each side of her head—measuring 14 mm on the right side, 12 mm on the left. It seemed unlikely that a single bump on the head could cause two separate bruises. So, what caused this?

CHAPTER 10

Wednesday, May 12th

Scot and I arrived at the hospital early in the morning. Kathy was lucid and unchanged from the day before.

"Hi, mom," Scot said. "How are you feeling?"

"Scotty!" she said in her usual way of greeting her son, whom she didn't see enough to satisfy her desire. "I love you, baby! Thanks for coming to see me!"

The nurse informed us that Dr. Syms had already been in to see Kathy. He found no signs of CSF leak around the implant site. He reiterated the need for her to manage the migraines and continue the use of the cochlear device.

Dr. Tejas Ranade, a young Neurology resident sporting a snappy bowtie, greeted us and gave us his assessment. "Based on the clinical picture alone, it doesn't appear to be a low pressure, or CSF Leak headache. This is because her headache doesn't change with leaning forward or laying down," he continued. "But given her subdural hematomas, a CSF leak headache would be reasonable etiology to evaluate."

"Huh? What the hell did you just say?" I thought to myself. "What is a low-pressure, CSF leak headache?" I stood there open-mouthed, shaking my head in the affirmative, pretending to understand. I realized I needed to ramp up my knowledge about such things.

It was the beginning of a steady stream of specialists, nurses, and technicians who would be providing their assessments and advice. Scot let the nurses and doctors know that he was a nurse. He would ask good questions and look like he was part of the team. I was proud of him and felt lucky to be able to watch him in action. It was like, 'bring your dad to work day.'

Someone arrived to give Kathy a verbal, mental acuity test. It seemed to go on and on and included math problems to be done in the head. I was even having trouble with the questions.

A rather attractive female doctor entered the room and caught my attention. "Hello, I'm Dr. Kerry Knievel." The stunned look on my face prompted a smile and response from the doctor. "Yeah, he's my great uncle." With that out of the way, it was down to business.

Dr. Knievel is a Neurologist specializing in migraine and headache disorders—couldn't have asked for anyone more suited. Why didn't we try to find someone like her weeks, months, or even years ago? I thought to myself.

"Let me explain what my resident Dr. Ranade was trying to convey," she began. "There is a concern that Kathy has an underlying CSF leak."

I recalled the term CSF while reading about subdural hematomas the night before. "Exactly what does all that mean?" I asked.

"Cerebro-Spinal Fluid, or CSF, surrounds the brain and the spinal cord and acts as a cushion to shock and injury. If there is a leak anywhere in the space, it could allow the brain to sag in the skull like a car with a flat tire," explained Dr. Knievel. "When that happens, bridging veins in the space could rupture and form hematomas on both sides."

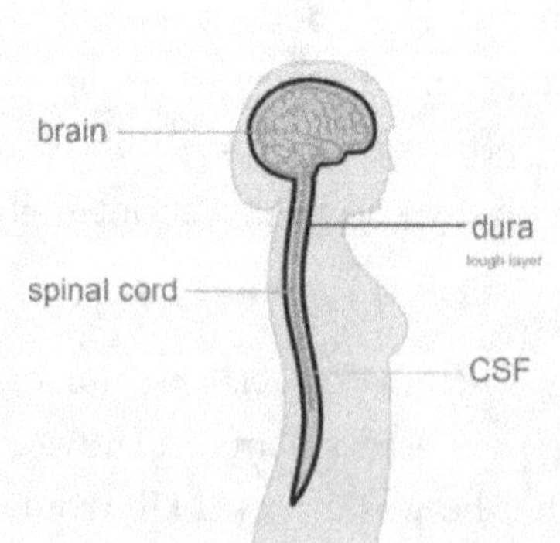

"Well, that makes sense," I responded cautiously.

I've ordered an MRI to look for spontaneous intracranial hypotension," she added. Whatever that is, at least we have a plan, I thought. "If this is the case, we'll do an epidermal blood patch as soon as possible."

I looked at Kathy, who was struggling and trying to comprehend what she was able to hear. By the time I thought to ask, "what the hell is a blood patch," Dr. Knievel was gone.

Why did Doctor Kneivel discount Kathy's claim that her pain remained the same sitting or lying down? Was it because she didn't report having bumped her head? Also, Kathy could be mistaken about her pain, which is subjective and could be misinterpreted by an individual.

The MRI was in continuous use with emergency priorities. In the meantime, they went ahead with a lumbar puncture (aka spinal tap) to measure her CSF pressure. This was a requirement before performing a blood patch.

The pressure is measured in the lumbar area of the spinal cord. It should be the same here as in the cranial area unless there is a blockage at the skull base.

They found elevated pressure, but they want to see the results of the MRI before doing anything else.

The opening pressure was measured at 32 cmH20. Normal-pressure for adults is in the range 7-18 or 5-25. Anything above 25 is cause for concern. But can high CSF pressure cause a CSF leak? Turns out the answer is yes, but rare. So, is there a CSF leak or not?

CHAPTER 11

Thursday, May 13th

Kathy was moved out of the ICU to a double room on the 5th floor. We began the waiting game for the MRI. Kathy was not able to eat.

Dr. Marc Staman came into our room and introduced himself. "I'm focusing on here, down," he pointed to his neck with both hands and lowered them down his abdomen. "I've been asked to examine Kathy for post-ICU management."

"Aah, Ok," I said.

The doctor did his examination but found nothing to add to solving the mystery. He recommended adding Dextrose to IV until she started eating again. That was it, and he left.

I stayed with Kathy, and we talked, though she had difficulty hearing, of course. Her headaches continued along with nausea and vomiting. She had trouble getting out of bed to go to the toilet. Even if she did get out of the bed, she could neither stand nor walk on her own. The nurse brought in a portable and set her down on it.

"What is taking so long for the MRI?" I asked the nurse. "This is so damn frustrating, waiting around to find out what's going on with Kathy."

"I agree," he responded, understanding our frustration. He began making calls to try to expedite.

Kathy turned to me with a desperate look on her face. It was the look of a confused child looking to her father for the truth; like that of a frightened life partner.

Without warning, she asked, "Am I going to die?"

I was stunned by her question. It triggered a plethora of thoughts in my head. Quickly I realized that Kathy and I were on the same mental plane of thought. At that moment, we both knew that death was a distinct possibility.

"Not on my watch, baby," I said as confidently as I could.

Friday, May 14th

Early morning Dr. Vaidyanathan ordered a CT scan to address changes in Kathy's mental status and her dilated eyes. The results indicated that her left hematoma had increased in size and density, and this may represent a new hemorrhage.

I texted Ryan to let him know the status. "Should I think about coming down, or are we not at that point yet," he asked. "Not yet," I replied.

We finally got an open slot for the MRI procedure—three full days after being admitted. Part of the reason for the delay, they said, was coordinating with a nurse to administer a sedative. Kathy was agitated and claustrophobic, and she needed to be sedated. The results of the morning CT scan probably helped to prioritize a slot.

I went down with Kathy and signed the authorization form around noon. The MRIs, one on her spine, the other on her brain, were performed. She was returned to the ICU by 2 pm. The report from the doctors was rather generic. "She handled the procedure well. We did not find the CSF leak," was all they said to me at the time.

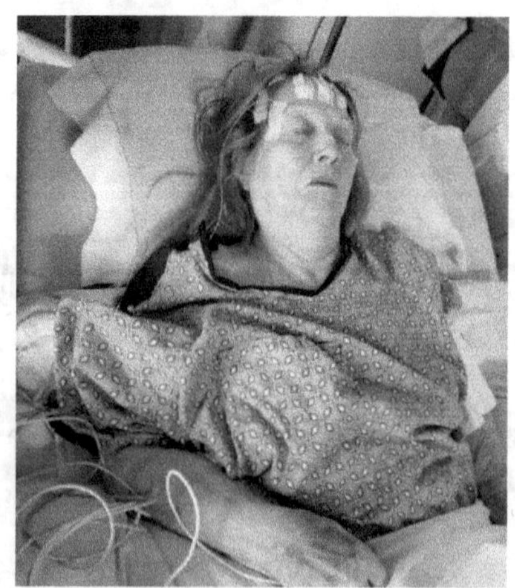

But there was more to the story that I wouldn't know until after I read the medical reports months later. The MRIs found that her brain had herniated; in other words, the brain was being forced into areas that it was not supposed to be. It's like squeezing a balloon or a squishy toy. The likely cause is the subdural hematomas pushing the brain down into the small opening in the skull through which the spinal cord passes. The process is called "coning," a severe condition with less than 40% survival rate. It's not hard to imagine this effects on the brain stem and the spinal cord. Could this be causing a blockage of the CSF flow, and the elevated pressure measured in the lumbar area is different from the area around the brain? Regardless, the doctors proceeded with the plan for a blood patch.

Doctors explained that an epidural blood patch is a procedure to patch a CSF leak somewhere in the sack surrounding the spinal cord and the brain. A small amount of the patient's blood is drawn, then injected into the lumbar region. The coagulation properties of the blood will attempt to stop the leak.

The procedure was performed in the ICU and completed around 5 pm. I left around 6 pm after Kathy appeared to be sleeping and resting comfortably.

...

While at home, I began to get text messages from Kathy.

"Can you come to see me," she texted me at 7:53 pm. "I can't, my love. I'll be back tomorrow," I responded immediately.

"Please see me ASAP. I miss you," at 9:59 pm. "Please come and. P," at 10:32 pm. "Come and I" included a selfie at 10:36 pm. "Please come and save me," along with another selfie at 10:39.

"Can't wait, my handsome guy," she texted at 11:35. "Good night, sweetheart," I responded immediately.

Saturday, May 15th

In the morning, the texts began as soon as she woke up.

"What a good pic of you. Please hurry and see me. I need you," Kathy sent at 9:02 am. "First meal I've had in days. Nasty," at 9:03 am. "What's happening with Eli? Is he ok?" at 9:05.

I responded that Eli was ok and that I was on my way

I was happy to read the morning texts. She seemed to be much more lucid. When I arrived, she was more aware and in a positive mood. She had EEG leads attached, which required her head to be shaved a little. But the blood patch seems to have made a positive difference. We were both optimistic.

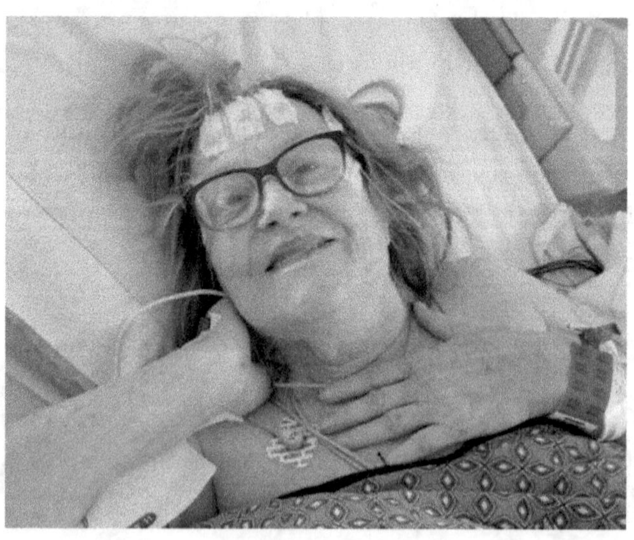

Kathy and the nurses were having difficulty communicating, even with her left side hearing aid inserted. I found an app called "Talk to Deaf Grandmother," which converted speech to text that Kathy could read the questions being asked of her.

It worked pretty well, and everyone was giddy with learning about the newfound and valuable tool.

It was a good day, and the question about dying seemed to have left both of our minds.

CHAPTER 12

Sunday, May 16th

"I am on the fifth floor now," Kathy texted me. "Come find me." "I'm on my way," I answered right away. "Yeah," she replied.

The fifth floor meant she was out of the ICU once more. A promising sign, I felt. When I arrived, the nurses told me her vitals were stable, but she was frail. She was seeing double and demonstrating short-term memory loss. The EEG leads were unattached.

We talked about our upcoming vacation to Florida, recalling our past trips there.

"Remember how we'd go to Publix and Sams Club to stock up for the week after we checked in?" Kathy said. "Then we would just hang out at the beach all week." "Yep, and we'd walk down to Armands Circle, to the shops and restaurants," I added.

These were very fond memories.

Monday, May 17th

Kathy was in stable condition, and her headaches were all but gone. The doctors were considering her discharge the next day, which I took with much suspicion. Even without knowing how severe her MRI results were, her condition didn't seem to be improving quickly enough. Her CT scans showed no change in the size of her hematomas. How could they think of releasing her when the condition that prompted her admission hasn't changed? All the focus was on the CSF leak that was never found. The blood patch improved Kathy's condition, and that's what mattered.

Kathy got a text message from our grandson Jack. "Hi Grandma, just checking in. I wanted you to know that I love you." "Yea Jackie, I love you too, sweetie," she responded.

She also was texting with her childhood friend, Jeannie. "Feeling much better, no headaches, don't know when can come home," she said to her.

This was the last time she communicated with anyone else.

Early evening Kathy began to appear agitated. She felt warm, and her headaches were getting much worse. She was seeing double as she had for the past several days. I got a wet cloth and tried to cool her down. Visitor hours were coming to an end, and I had to leave.

"I love you, sweetheart," I told her, then left for home. This was the last time I communicated with Kathy.

When I got home, I prepared some frozen food and watched some TV.

Unknown to me at the time, doctors performed a CT scan of her head at 11:22 pm. The details of this were again in the medical reports that I read months later. The CT scan found "No significant change; no new hemorrhage; continued bilateral subdural." But what was significant from the report was the stated reason for the exam. AMS—Altered Mental Status. The term seems rather generic to most of us. But when a doctor refers to AMS, it may point to the onset of delirium, dementia, or coma. The CT scan showed nothing, but the diagnosis remained nonetheless. Urgent action was required.

CHAPTER 13

Tuesday, May 18th

My cellphone rang at 12:15 am and woke me up from a dead sleep.

"This is Doctor Mirzadeh. Your wife has taken a turn for the worse. We're going to have to do an emergency craniotomy to relieve the pressure in her brain. We need to get your permission to do this procedure," the doctor said to me.

Another person got on the phone who explained what they intended to do and asked me to repeat what they said, which I did the best that I could.

"Do you authorize this procedure?" he asked. "Yes, of course," I responded.

As I ended the call, my mind again began racing. The thought of Kathy dying returned to me again as a real possibility, if not a certainty. I laid back in my bed and thought about Kathy being so upset while her beloved dog "Sissy" was dying in her arms. I began to sob and soon fell asleep.

I was awakened by a phone call once again at 4:07 am. I immediately thought the worst; that Kathy had died. It was Doctor Mirzadeh calling to tell me they decided to take a less drastic course of action. He explained the procedure—burr hole drainage surgery and again turned me over to his assistant for my verbal authorization, which I did. It seemed to be positive news, and I went back to sleep.

They intubated her to protect her airways since she exhibited some respiratory distress. Immediately the doctors inserted a central venous catheter (or central line) because the existing IV tube was inadequate.

They called me later to tell me the procedure went well, but I knew this was only in relative terms. Kathy was very sick, and I knew that in my heart.

I visited Kathy in the morning and found her with her head shaved, even more, exposing the ugly stitches and the tubes. She was intubated, and I was concerned because I had heard that it was almost a death sentence when you are intubated. I didn't know if she was suffering, and that bothered me. All I could do was pray that she was not.

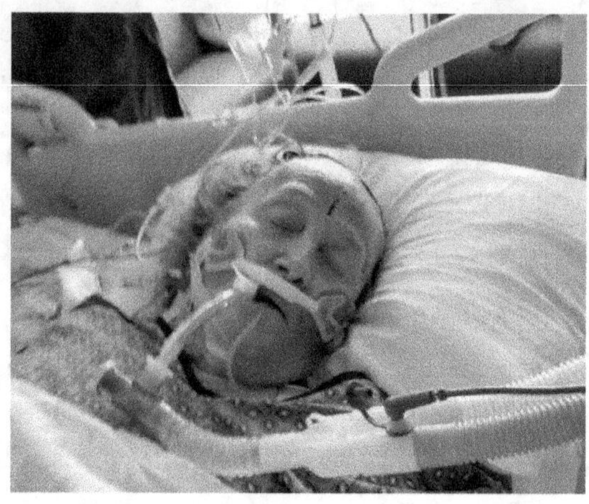

...

I spent the day with her lying on the couch by the window and watched the medical helicopters fly to the roof and land above us. I wondered if her present condition was caused more by the burr hole surgery or by the hematomas. Was the treatment worse than the disease?

They were giving Kathy so many medications, doctors decided to insert a Central Line into the right internal jugular. Another tube in her body.

Today was much different than the day before. The idea that Kathy might be dying became firmly planted in my mind. My son Ryan decided to come down to Phoenix. I hoped I didn't make a mistake in telling him not to come down earlier when he suggested.

As I was driving out of the parking garage, I called Ryan to give him an update. "I don't like seeing her like this," I said to him as I wept.

"Hang in there, Dad. I'll be there tomorrow," he said to me.

CHAPTER 14

Wednesday, May 19th

When I arrived in the morning, Kathy was still intubated and resting. It was hard for me to see my wife lying there with the tubes coming out of her head and mouth. I laid down on the couch and began to process—everything.

A nurse came over to me to see how I was doing. She confided in me that Kathy's condition is a mystery to the staff. At first, I thought, at least I'm not alone in thinking that. But then I quickly realized that this was not good news. I'm allowed to not know what was going on, but you don't have that privilege. You are supposed to know what's going on. I didn't say out loud what I was thinking, but I began to realize that my frustration was morphing to anger. I thanked her for her honesty.

I left for the airport to pick up Ryan around 3 pm, and we went right back to the hospital. While I was gone, the doctors did another CT scan to see any change in the hematomas since they inserted the tubes. There was no significant change to report.

They planned to do another MRI later in the day to continue their hunt for the CSF leak.

Medical records show they were using a more advanced technique called MRI myelography, which can help to localize a CSF leak in the 'thecal' (or Dural) sac. They were pulling out the big guns.

Ryan and I left after they took Kathy down to do the MRIs around 7:30.

E.W. Borgoyne

Thursday, May 20th

Ryan, Scot, and I arrived in the morning, and doctors delivered some bad news and some even worse news. The bad news—the MRIs revealed no evidence of CSF leaks. The CT scan uncovered the worst part.

Doctor Mirzadeh told us the CT scan showed that Kathy had a stroke. "This is in the area of the midbrain that affects hearing and sight.", he explained.

Medical records provide more detail. They missed the stroke in the scan they did the day before. It was a Posterior Cerebral Artery Stroke. Causing loss of ability to understand or express speech, executive dysfunction, decreased level of consciousness, and memory impairment.

It took a few seconds for this to sink in. Hearing and sight? "Oh, my God!" I cried out. "She could be blind and deaf?" There seemed to be no end to the mounting medical challenges that Kathy was having to bear. I leaned in next to Kathy's partially shaved head and wept. I was feeling overwhelming regret. "I am so sorry, baby, that I can't fix this," I said to her.

Kathy's brothers and sisters came to the hospital that afternoon, but they couldn't see her. I didn't know this, but there was a two-person per day limit on the number of visitors allowed. We were lucky they allowed Ryan, Scot, and me to be there at the same time. The nurses and staff seem to have bent the rules for us, but they drew the line when half a dozen more visitors waited in the lobby. It was odd to me because just that day, the CDC announced that those who are vaccinated no longer need to wear masks or social distance in indoor settings. But these were strange times, and I was grateful that this was happening last year when no visitors were allowed.

Back in the ICU, I found myself overcome with emotions. The emotions quickly changed as if switching channels on the television.

I was angry at Dr. Syms for what he did to my wife. This was all his fault, I thought. Though I couldn't quite put my finger on what it was that he did wrong, he was a convenient target of opportunity. Then there was the hospital. Why did it take three whole days for her to get the MRI that might have shed light on her condition sooner? Next in line for mental flogging was the staff, the doctors, and the nurses, who saw this as a mystery. Really? And, why did you drag your feet in telling me the truth?

I was fixated and staring at nothing in particular. I shook my head to clear my thoughts and began staring in another direction. Almost immediately, my emotions switched to denial.

"This isn't happening," I thought. Maybe I'm dreaming all of this. I thought back over the past few weeks and realized I hadn't grasped the seriousness of Kathy's condition. My denial had been trickling in all the while, and now it was a flood. I was numb; it was a null emotion.

Once again, I shook my head to clear my thoughts and began staring in another direction. This time it was acceptance. I began to think about what my new life will be like without Kathy. Could I learn to live with this new reality? Of course, I could, I thought. I became subsumed into a sense of independence. I could do whatever I wanted. Eat whatever I wanted. Go wherever I wanted.

My channel switched back to anger, this time directed at Kathy. She was always a pain in the ass about everything, I thought. So picky about what to have for dinner. "I don't like meatballs; I don't like mushrooms unless they're chopped up;" Blah, blah, blah. It was an endless list of forbidden menu items. Why do you make my life so difficult, I thought?

The emotional swings seemed to have continued for an hour or so as the thoughts ran through my head. "Why are you leaving me alone to take care of our grandkids?" "Her body is worn out, it's her time." "Why didn't I take her condition more seriously?" "Why are you leaving me before we finished our life goals?"

It became a delicate balance between holding on to hope and letting go of what I was dealing with in my mind. An image began to form of seeing her in the rearview mirror as I slowly drove down the road. A new relationship was developing in my head, one in which I would only remember the good things.

I thought I was losing my mind.

Therapists call it anticipatory grief.

CHAPTER 15

Friday, May 21st

It was an easy drive to the hospital from the house. At Gilbert Road, I just get on the 60 west to I-10 West, then take the 3rd Street exit, north to Thomas, past Dr. Sym's office, turn west to 3rd Avenue. It was straightforward when one or both of my sons were with me since we could take HOV lane to 3rd Street without thinking about anything. With all of its electronic smarts, I believe my Camry Hybrid automatically knew the way by this time.

On the way in and out of the ICU, we walked past the Bret Michaels Hospitality and Music Room. Decorated in a music theme featuring some of his music memorabilia, it was a relaxation area for patients and families. Bret opened this facility in 2012 after being treated for and surviving a subarachnoid hemorrhage (below the protective brain layers) in 2010. This was similar to what Kathy was dealing with, except hers was subdural (within the protective brain layers). I wasn't a fan, but I remember the event very well. I never went into the room, which was locked. Passing the room each day gave me some hope, but any hope was steadily fading.

Saturday, May 22nd

The doctors discovered some activity in her EEG data. It was a rare lateralized rhythmic delta activity, the nurse told me. At this point, every new piece of information was alarming. It indicated a high risk of a seizure in a critically ill patient. They kept the EEG led on and continued to monitor, and it turned out to be nothing.

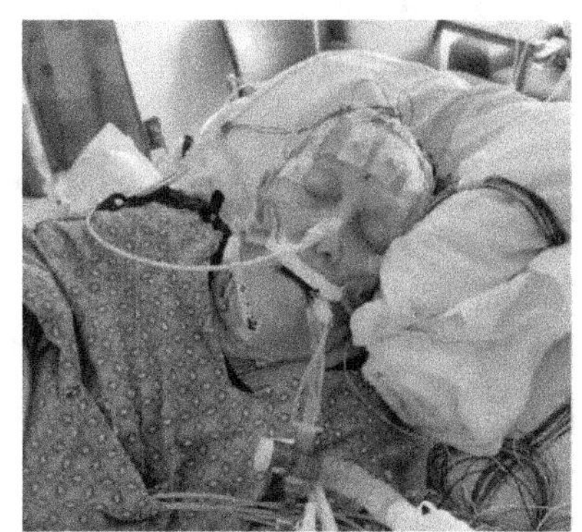

Sunday, May 23rd

I took Ryan to the airport early in the morning. Scot also returned to his home in Payson. There was no change in Kathy's status, and I decided to stay home for the day. I watched some of the PGA championship hoping for another win by Phil Mickelson. He pulled it off in the end. He is a decent guy and an ASU alum to boot. Kathy loved to watch golf on TV. She never played anything other than goofy golf.

Monday, May 24th

Listening to the news on the way into the hospital, I learned that the CDC is looking into a small number of teens who've experienced heart problems after getting the COVID vaccine. Could the vaccine have caused Kathy's condition, I continued to ask myself? Maybe I should have suggested to Kathy to wait on the vaccine for a while. But for how long? And what do I know anyway? Besides, she's not having heart problems. The second-guessing was driving me virtually crazy.

When I arrived in the ICU, I walked over to Kathy and whispered into her ear, "I'm so sorry I can't fix this, Baby." I rested my head next to hers. I gently wrapped my arms around her while being careful not to disturb the tubes and leads. Then I wept.

The doctors decided to do a craniotomy that afternoon to remove the thickened blood. The tubes they put into her head almost a week ago aren't reducing the size of her hematomas. It was a risky procedure that required the removal of a section of bone from the skull to get access to the brain.

I assumed my usual position on the couch, lying and waiting. The room, and the entire hospital, was cold. The nurses continued to supply me with warm blankets and treated me with comfort and respect.

My thoughts began to return to that dark valley of mixed emotions. This time, acceptance was the dominant one. I began to plan Kathy's memorial for when, not if she finally passed.

I also contacted an attorney who was successful in helping my daughter in the past. It was a preemptive move and wasn't seriously considering any legal action at this time. He simply told me to collect as much information as possible.

CHAPTER 16

Tuesday, May 25th

Early that morning, doctors performed a craniotomy on Kathy. After I arrived, the nurses put me in touch by phone with Dr. Zaman Mirzadeh, who operated.

"We removed a very thick subdural membrane that had been blocking the drainage tubes," he said to me. "I'm optimistic." I thought to myself, optimistic, like when the fire department tells you they saved the chimney after your house burnt down.

Her head was shaved entirely on the right side with an ugly scar and tubes draining into a plastic pouch resting on the floor. She was gasping, trying to remove the lines in her arms, and the nurses had to restrain her.

Later I allowed a Chaplain to sit with me and talk. He offered his services a few days earlier, but this time I was ready. I sat and listened to his comforting voice of reality. He told me that I would have to make tough decisions that could affect my family emotionally and financially. I immediately knew what he meant—Kathy would not survive without continuous long-term medical attention and primary care.

By mid-afternoon, doctors asked for my permission to do an Arterial Line Insertion because of the need for frequent blood draws. Another needle and tube emanating from her body.

My hope continued ratcheting down.

Wednesday, May 26th

Kathy was now awake but unresponsive to commands. Doctors don't understand why she isn't responding to commands. Nurses were telling me that this could take a long time. It takes time to heal a brain injury. You didn't need to be a brain surgeon to understand that was an understatement. They moved her to a chair to improve her circulation. But soon, they returned her back to her bed.

Maybe it was my imagination, but it seemed that everyone in the ICU knew how this story would end. Nurses would pass the room, glancing slightly in our direction, then whisper something to a peer. Some would come in and talk to me in such a way I felt they wanted to tell me more but couldn't.

Thursday, May 27th

Doctors removed her intubation. She was awake but still unresponsive.

Her eyes were staring into space as she struggled to sit up in her bed as if she was trying to get up. I waved my hand in front of her face. I placed her hearing aid in her good ear and tried to get her attention. There was nothing. From my perspective, she was completely deaf and now blind. Putting my hand in hers, she squeezed it firmly as if she wanted desperately to tell me something. The nurse reminded me that it would take a long time to recover from a brain injury. I knew she was trying to give me some sense of hope.

What goes on in a person's mind when suddenly thrust into a dark and silent world? Was she aware of where she was? Was she crying inside, wondering where I was and why I wasn't helping her? Did she think she was dead? I recorded a video of her, and it is hard to watch.

The doctors and nurses never mentioned the word, but I concluded she was in vegetative state; unconscious with no awareness of herself or her surroundings. I prayed that she was not suffering.

I stared straight ahead in a confused state. Turning to the left, I saw darkness; to the right was anticipation. I was full of emotion and desire.

It occurred to me that I hadn't been bargaining, as is typical during a state of grief. I gave up bargaining a long time ago. I realized how selfish it was to ask God to "pass this class" or "get this job." "Please, I'll do this or that." What a selfish person I used to be. Praying for outcomes that are in my own control. Now I prayed for things that were entirely out of my control. This time it would be for Kathy's comfort.

Friday, May 28th, 2021

The cochlear implant was removed in the morning to get an unobstructed MRI. They found no abnormalities that might have caused her issues. She remained intubated for the upcoming MRI.

Saturday, May 29th, 2021

The MRI was scheduled for the morning, and there was nothing I could do at the hospital. I attended the memorial for my friend Ken who died in December from a long illness. It was a beautiful celebration of Ken's life. I remembered the positive impact he and his wife Carol had on my life when they taught me serenity. I began to think about Kathy's memorial.

There was only a small circle of friends who knew about Kathy's condition at this time. One of them said to me it was so nice of me to attend Ken's memorial. But the isolation wasn't a solution. Besides, I explained to her that we have to live our lives as usual as we can during times like this. Honoring a friend is a normal thing to do.

That evening I had dinner with my friend Ted who drove down from Reno for the memorial. I almost allowed isolation to consume my emotions and stay home, but I chose normalcy.

Sunday, May 30th

I met with the radiologist Dr. Dinko Plasto who very patiently explained the results of the MRI. He even drew a diagram on the whiteboard. The MRI confirmed a stroke in the mid-brain. It was an Ischemic Stroke in which the blood vessel became blocked, in this case by her sagging brain. I understood what 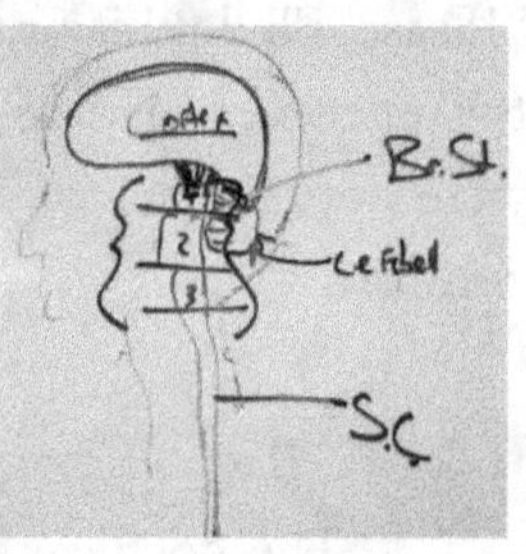 he was saying. "But what does this mean for her—what is her prognosis?" I asked. He told me I would need to talk to the neurosurgeon.

Monday, May 31st

When I arrived, I insisted on talking with the neurosurgeon face to face. Dr. Zaman Mirzadeh came to the room and spoke very frankly.

"It is unlikely she would ever be able to function independently," were the words he said to me.

A strange sense of calm came over me.

CHAPTER 17

Tuesday, June 1st, 2021

Scot and I made our final trip to the ICU in the morning. Kathy was awake and sitting up in her bed but grasping and staring expressionlessly. The only sound she made was her labored breathing. I leaned over, kissed her, and told her that I loved her. My heart was breaking as I contemplated what I was about to do.

Scot knew what had to be done, and I took the cue from him. "I want to change my wife's code to DNR," I said. A new sense of reality came over me as I thought about what those 3 letters meant— Do Not Resuscitate. The patient would ordinarily request this, but I had the medical power of attorney to make this request on her behalf. I showed the living will outlining Kathy's final wishes to one of the nurses.

An administrator came to me with a list of Hospice choices. In-home Hospice was out of the question with small grandchildren to take care of. I chose a Hospice location close to our home for Kathy's final care before her inevitable passing. I thought about how many times I heard Lin Sue Cooney talk about Hospice of the Valley on TV and never thought I would need them.

Once the decision was made, things moved very quickly, as if they were trying to free up her room as soon as possible. I was signing forms; nurses were unplugging cords and devices from Kathy. Then they moved her to a gurney. A rash of calls was made informing the family of our decision.

We left for home. I got a call from Hospice telling me that Kathy has been checked in and is resting comfortably. I went to bed; my granddaughter Kaili came into my room and saw me crying.

E.W. Borgoyne

Tuesday, June 2nd, 2021

Dobson Home in Chandler was one of three Hospice of the Valley locations in the East Valley of Phoenix. First built in 1939 as a family residence and sheep farm of the Dobson family. It was remodeled and opened in 2004 with eleven private rooms. Each room has access to an outside patio area. We were lucky to have been able to find this treasured sanctuary in the desert.

I went to see Kathy early in the morning. The nurses placed a knitted cap on Kathy's head to cover her ugly scars.

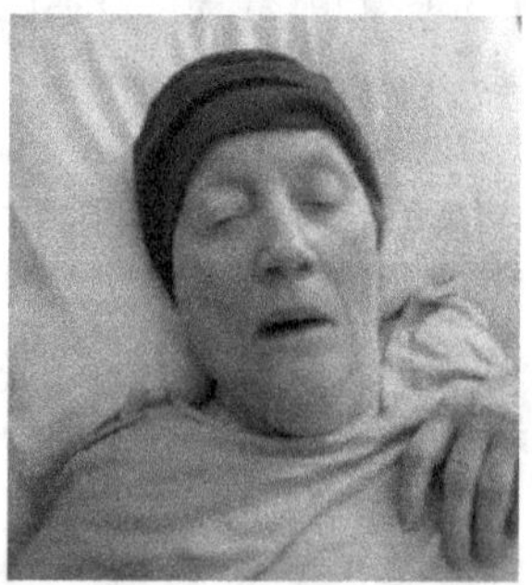

The people at Hospice were thoughtful and caring. The doctor told me she is recommending that her case be reviewed by the state medical review board.

Untethered Love

Most of the Banta family residing in Arizona came to see Kathy. We shared stories and laughed and cried.

I met Chaplain Ken, who worked there. He was terrific, and he offered to help at any services we planned.

Wednesday, June 3rd

Scot and I spent much of the day with her.

"Mom is exhibiting Cheyne Stokes breathing," Scot said. "She doesn't have long."

It was the last day he would see his mother alive.

CHAPTER 18

Frightened of the thing that I've become

Tuesday, June 5th, 2021

It was the first day of the rest of my life without Kathy. The anger from the night before had left my heart, and only numbness remained. I acquired a new label—widower. A mild state of shock came over me as I thought about this. I felt the same sort of shock when I changed labels from 'single' to 'married' almost forty-five years earlier. Our vows bound us together to deal with the better things and worse things that life threw at us in marriage. In death, our love becomes untethered to these distractions.

There was much to be done, and that kept me out of a state of depression. The house was in roughly the same condition three weeks earlier when I took Kathy to Mercy Gilbert. Her things were where she left them, and I realized it was up to me what to do with all her stuff. The house was an absolute mess, but first things first.

The doctor at Hospice informed me that the state medical examiner refused the case. I called them to find out why; they simply did not have the resources to pursue this. They told me I could request an autopsy, but this would cost $10K or more. I authorized Hospice to release Kathy's body to the mortuary for cremation.

A few days later, the mortuary returned her ashes along with a death certificate. Cause of death, "ischemic cerebrovascular infarcts due to spontaneous bilateral subdural hematomas." I already knew all this from talking with the doctors, but the root cause question remained unanswered. I had already requested the medical records during the time Kathy was in the hospital. When I have the time, I will pour over these and try to get some answers. But first things first.

Early June

Friends sent us gifts of food like fruit, snacks and even some chicken soup! These were welcome gifts and were much appreciated.

My daughter Ashley and I began planning Kathy's celebration of life. I could not imagine having a standard funeral service just days after a death. A proper celebration had to be well thought out. We picked a date based on the availability of a venue and to give people enough time to plan to come out. There was no getting around the fact it would be in the middle of the Arizona summer. Saturday, July 24th was the date.

We divided up the planning and got to work. A friend of mine provided a beautiful venue for us at no cost. I ordered announcements and got them sent out. Again, first things first. I started work on a slide presentation, a eulogy, and a song playlist of Kathy's favorite artists like Steely Dan, Bruce Hornsby, and others.

Ashley was in charge of the food, table decorations, flowers, and per her suggestion, homing doves.

"Homing doves?? What the hell are homing doves?" I asked.

"It's a dove release symbolizing the release of the spirit," she explained to me. "Mom would appreciate that because she is very spiritual."

Mid-June

I began the process of sorting through Kathy's clothes and possessions. It would be a slow, deliberate process. I didn't want to make a regretful mistake.

I started with her box of memorabilia that contained pictures, awards, recognitions, diplomas, and other things of that sort. Some of these items I pulled out for display at her celebration. Others I threw out. I felt a sense of responsibility for her legacy and didn't make these decisions lightly.

Her doll restoration business included a large inventory of dolls, doll parts, and clothing. There were heads, arms, legs, torsos, tiny shoes, undergarments, you name it. I logged onto her eBay account *startemple*. She was so proud of her 1,145 ratings, 100% positive feedback. I was a stranger in her domain. She had developed a clientele, and I didn't want to upset that in any way. "My wife passed away, and I'm selling her inventory," I stated in the listings. Everything auctioned off quickly.

Early July

There was a sense of acceptance creeping into my heart. I knew that cleaning out Kathy's personal belongings as part of that. But I began to realize that this new reality is a permanent thing, and I had to learn to live with it.

The reality was that I was a 70-year-old widower. Will I ever love another woman? Will I ever have sex again? I was frightened by this reality. I wanted to get a head start.

After a couple of rough starts, I joined an online dating site— one you pay for. Turns out the free ones can create a lot of chaos in your life.

My profile included "recently widowed," and as expected, that attracted women in similar situations. I was surprised by the number of responses I got and realized I was not alone. It was very strange to me to be meeting up for coffee or drinks with another woman. I felt I was in an alternate universe. Conversations would eventually turn to the question of how long since my wife passed. "Seriously? Your wife died only a month ago, and you're over it?"

Well, no, I'm not over it, I thought to myself. But there was this need to jumpstart my new life. And Kathy and I always encouraged each other to find someone after the other passed. I decided I needed more time to sort things out, and I shut down my profile—at least temporarily.

CHAPTER 19

Saturday, July 24th

like a warm blanket of love

A cool monsoon rain greeted the guests the morning of Kathy's Celebration of Life. The temperatures were hovering in the triple digits throughout most of July. On Friday, a wet summer monsoon came through, dropping the temperature to 84 degrees. On this morning, the temperature dropped to 81 degrees—the coolest day of the summer. It seemed to be divine intervention. It was perfect, and I was happy for the out-of-town guests.

They came from Pennsylvania, Florida, Washington, Texas, California, and Nevada. Kathy's best childhood friend Jeannie planned to come from Utah, but the airline canceled her flight at the last moment. My two brothers and their spouses came from the east. Most of Kathy's family were there, and many of our long-time friends were. My high school friends Carol, Ted and Maryellen, were there. I thanked Ted for coming back from Reno, Nevada, after he was just here a few weeks ago for Ken's memorial. He said something I will remember forever. "You are my friend, and I wanted to be there for you."

Chaplain Ken from Hospice led the service just as we had asked. Kathy was not a religious person, but she was spiritual and believed in God.

I shared my memories in a eulogy that I spent the past several weeks preparing. Then others shared their memories. Many talked about how Kathy unselfishly helped them in their time of need. I heard about the silly things she did with her nephews. Most of the stories I had heard before, but this time I got "the rest of the story" never shared with me before. "It was like a warm blanket of love," someone shared with me privately.

Another divine intervention happened around 11 am that morning. It had been raining steadily all morning, and the birdman said the doves couldn't be released if it was raining. Just as the time for the event arrived, the rains suddenly quit, and the skies cleared.

My oldest grandson and my granddaughter participated in the ceremony. I have to admit it was beautiful. It wouldn't have happened without my daughter's female touch.

CHAPTER 20

August

I've come to learn recently, even before all this happened, that love is not an emotion. It's a spiritual force like the natural forces of gravity and magnetism. Once it gets hold, it doesn't let go, even after death. In life, love is shrouded by all sorts of emotions: sadness, happiness, anger, fear, and sometimes even hate. When a loved one dies, memories of the bad times fade away, and the good ones remain. A new relationship is formed, one without the negative strings that are attached in life. This is what I call *Unthethored Love*.

I've learned that I can begin a new-normal and happy life, with Kathy still part of it in my new relationship with her.

I reactivated my profile on the dating site and began to date. Seeing other women was something I never thought I would be doing again, but it is part of my new-normal world. I have no expectations, and I've met some new and fascinating friends.

I continue the process of shaping my new world: discarding the horrible stuff and keeping the good; building on my relationship with my children and grandchildren; meeting new people; traveling, and writing. Perhaps I can even come to put the medical mystery of Kathy's death behind me.

August 12th

Ryan called me and told me about something his wife Nicole suddenly remembered while watching a movie that had a scene about head traumas. She recalled Kathy telling her, a few weeks before anything happened, that she was picking up Eli's toys, she stood up and hit the top of her head on a cabinet door very hard!

"Ohhhh, really?" I said curiously.

AFTERWORD

Kathy died from a stroke caused by hematomas pressing down and pinching off blood vessels to her mid-brain. That much is certain. But what caused the hematomas? Was it a CSF leak that allowed the brain to settle, causing bridging veins to be stretched and torn, or was it a bump to the head?

My daughter-in-law, Nicole's recollection about Kathy bumping her head, triggered a similar memory. I tried to bring this into focus, but it remained only a vague thought. Maybe it was the power of suggestion and the desire to understand the root cause. But Kathy or I would have recalled this when we were asked about it. Wouldn't we?

What if she had bumped her head, and we told the doctors from the start. Would that have led the doctors in a different direction, other than the elusive CSF leak?

I honestly think it has nothing to do with the cochlear implant nor the COVID vaccine.

Whatever the root cause, we will probably never know. It will remain a medical mystery.

ABOUT THE AUTHOR

Ernest (Ernie) William Borgoyne was born in Braddock, PA, in 1951. His family moved to Monroeville, PA, when he was six years old, and he lived there through High School and two years of community college. He moved to Tempe, AZ, to attend Arizona State University, receiving Bachelor's and Master's degrees in Engineering. He worked as an engineer for Motorola and Honeywell Aerospace before retiring in 2017. He and his late wife Kathy Ann (Banta) Borgoyne have three children and four grandchildren.

In 2019 he published his first book—*The Faithful Patriot: Soul of the American Revolution*. In 2020 he published his second book—*Slovak Americans of Braddock Pa.: the Soul of the Monongahela Valley*.

www.ingramcontent.com/pod-product-compliance
Lightning Source LLC
Chambersburg PA
CBHW050048260726

48658CB00005B/1832